Sisters
of the Heart

Artwork by
Sandra Kuck

HARVEST HOUSE PUBLISHERS

EUGENE, OREGON

$\mathcal{M}$y sister! With that thrilling word

Let thoughts unnumbered wildly spring!

What echoes in my heart are stirred,

While thus I touch the trembling string.

MARGARET DAVIDSON

For there is no friend like a sister
In calm or stormy weather;
To cheer one on the tedious way,
To fetch one if one goes astray,
To lift one if one totters down,
To strengthen whilst one stands.

CHRISTINA ROSSETTI

Sisters are for sharing laughter and wiping tears.

AUTHOR UNKNOWN

My sister took a quieter road than I did, as a nurse, wife, and mother. In my mother's failing days I saw my sister shine and take charge. With enormous appreciation for gifts and talents I did not possess, I saw my sister in a new light. She had always quietly been there, right beside me, but mostly in my shadow. How blessed I felt that God had given me a sister who was not only a shoulder to lean on, but who could take the lead when I was unable. My sister will always have a special place in my heart.

ALDA ELLIS

Sisters touch your heart in ways no other could. Sisters share...their hopes, their fears, their love, everything they have. Real friendship springs from their special bonds.

CARRIE BAGWELL

Chance made us sisters, hearts made us friends.

AUTHOR UNKNOWN

Amy stirred, and sighed in her sleep; and, as if eager to begin at once to mend her fault, Jo looked up with an expression on her face which it had never worn before.

"I let the sun go down on my anger; I wouldn't forgive her, and today, if it hadn't been for Laurie, it might have been too late! How could I be so wicked?" said Jo, half aloud, as she leaned over her sister, softly stroking the wet hair scattered on the pillow.

As if she heard, Amy opened her eyes, and held out her arms, with a smile that went straight to Jo's heart. Neither said a word, but they hugged one another close, in spite of the blankets, and everything was forgiven and forgotten in one hearty kiss.

LOUISA MAY ALCOTT
Little Women

Whatever you do they will love you; even if they don't love you they are connected to you till you die.
You can be boring and tedious with sisters, whereas you have to put on a good face with friends.

DEBORAH MOGGACH

Sisters are special
From young ones to old.
God gave me a sister
More precious than gold.

AUTHOR UNKNOWN

Sure, Rob's a girl all right, and I'm mighty glad of it. I wouldn't...have Rob anything else—I should say not. Name's Roberta, you know, after father. She's a peach of a sister, I tell you. Ruth's all right, too, of course, but she's different. She's a girl all through. But Rob's half boy, or—I should say there's just enough boy about her to make her exactly right, if you know what I mean."

GRACE S. RICHMOND
The Twenty-Fourth of June

To have a loving relationship
with a sister is not simply to
have a buddy or a confidant—
it is to have a soulmate for life.

VICTORIA SECUNDA

There is a space within
sisterhood for likeness
and difference, for the
subtle differences that
challenge and delight.

CHRISTINE DOWNING

The love that grew with us from our cradles never knew diminutions from time or distance. Other ties were formed, but they did not supersede or weaken this.

CHARLOTTE ELIZABETH TONNA

In thee my soul shall own combined: The sister and the friend.

CATHERINE KILLIGREW

If you don't understand how a woman could both
love her sister dearly and want to wring her neck at
the same time, then you were probably an only child.

LINDA SUNSHINE

*O*ften, of pleasant afternoons, the two
would drink their black coffee, seated upon
the stone-flagged portico whose canopy was
the blue sky of Louisiana. They loved to sit
there in the silence, with only each other
and the sheeny, prying lizards for company,
talking of the old times and planning for the
new; while light breezes stirred the tattered
vines high up among the columns, where
owls nested.

KATE CHOPIN
Ma'ame Pelagie

There's a special kind of freedom sisters enjoy—freedom to share innermost thoughts,
to ask a favor, to show their true feelings—the freedom to simply be themselves.

AUTHOR UNKNOWN

She is the bowl of golden water
which brims but never overflows.

VIRGINIA WOOLF

*Sisters function as
safety nets in a chaotic
world simply by being
there for each other.*

CAROL SALINE

*T*he sisters had been sitting upstairs, looking out at the beautiful grounds of the old place, and marvelling at the violets, which lifted their heads from every possible cranny about the house, and talking over the cordiality which they had been receiving by those upon whom they had no claim, and they were filled with amiable satisfaction. Life looked attractive...They descended the stairs together, with arms clasped about each other's waists, and as they did so presented a placid and pleasing sight. They entered their drawing-room with the intention of brewing a cup of tea, and drinking it in calm sociability in the twilight.

ELIA W. PEATTIE
A Grammatical Ghost

A sister is a little bit of childhood that can never be lost.

MARION C. GARRETTY

Sisters are always drying their hair. Locked into rooms, alone, they pose at the mirror, shoulders bare, trying this way and that their hair, or fly importunate down the stair to answer the telephone.

PHYLLIS McGINLEY

I had two sisters, and we would love to get dressed up and pretend that we were chic, sophisticated ladies. And I think that was a great sort of preparation, in a way.

SUZANNE FARRELL

The best thing about having a sister was that I always had a friend.

CALI RAE TURNER

Elder sisters never can
do younger ones justice!

CHARLOTTE M. YONGE

For the younger sisters, we always look up to the older sisters
because they're always ahead of us and they always win.

SERENA WILLIAMS

*W*hen she bid her sister goodnight she looked on her with her large…wild eyes, till something of her old human affections seemed to gather there, and they slowly filled with tears, which dropped one after the other on her homely dress as she gazed in her sister's face.

JOSEPH SHERIDAN LE FANU
A Legend of Cappercullen

Having a sister is like having a best friend you can't get rid of. You know whatever you do, they'll still be there.

AMY LI

There can be no situation in life in which the conversation of my dear sister will not administer some comfort to me.

MARY WORLEY MONTAGU

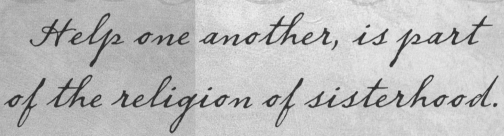

Help one another, is part of the religion of sisterhood.

LOUISA MAY ALCOTT

*G*odber's has come," announced Sadie, issuing out of the pantry. She had seen the man pass the window. That meant the cream puffs had come. Godber's were famous for their cream puffs. Nobody ever thought of making them at home.

"Bring them in and put them on the table, my girl," ordered cook. Sadie brought them in and went back to the door. Of course Laura and Jose were far too grown-up to really care about such things. All the same, they couldn't help agreeing that the puffs looked very attractive. Very. Cook began arranging them, shaking off the extra icing sugar.

"Don't they carry one back to all one's parties?" said Laura.

"I suppose they do," said practical Jose, who never liked to be carried back. "They look beautifully light and feathery, I must say."

"Have one each, my dears," said cook in her comfortable voice. "Yer ma won't know."

Oh, impossible. Fancy cream puffs so soon after breakfast. The very idea made one shudder. All the same, two minutes later Jose and Laura were licking their fingers with that absorbed inward look that only comes from whipped cream.

KATHERINE MANSFIELD
The Garden Party

An older sister helps one remain half child, half woman.

AUTHOR UNKNOWN

To the outside world we all grow old. But not to brothers and sisters. We know each other as we always were. We know each other's hearts. We share private family jokes. We remember family feuds and secrets, family griefs and joys. We live outside the touch of time.

CLARA ORTEGA

How do people make it through life without a sister?

SARA CORPENING

Sisterhood is powerful.

ROBIN MORGAN

An older sister is a friend
and defender—a listener,
conspirator, a counselor
and a sharer of delights.
And sorrows too.

PAM BROWN

The mildest, drowsiest sister has been known
to turn tiger if her sibling is in trouble.

CLARA ORTEGA

31

$\mathcal{S}$he is your mirror, shining back at you with a world of possibilities. She is your witness, who sees you at your worst and best, and loves you anyway. She is your partner in crime, your midnight companion, someone who knows when you are smiling, even in the dark. She is your teacher, your defense attorney, your personal press agent, even your shrink. Some days, she's the reason you wish you were an only child.

BARBARA ALPERT